God
Loves you!
John 3:16
Pat Day
5-1-12

The KENTUCKY DERBY

Churchill DOWNS

PRESENTED BY THE KENTUCKY DERBY MUSEUM

Timeless · Tradition · Heritage

Written by:
Katherine Veitschegger, Curator of Collections
Kentucky Derby Museum
Edited by: Wendy Treinen, Director of Communications
Kentucky Derby Museum

Acknowledgements
Special thanks to the following individuals and
organizations for their support:
Angie Fleitz
Christine George
Sam Thomas
Dick Duncan
Bud Kameniske
University of Louisville
Keeneland Library
The *Courier-Journal*
Churchill Downs
Kinetic Corporation
Kentucky Office of Creative Services

© 2009 Designed in USA by Terrell Creative
Printed in China • 09B0001

ISBN-13: 978-1-56944-390-3

The History *of The Kentucky Derby and Churchill Downs*

On the first Saturday in May, all eyes turn towards the Kentucky Derby. The race has become legend and it is known worldwide as the "Greatest Two Minutes in Sports™." Ladies in hats, men tucked in seersucker suits with mint juleps in hand; the crowd waits with suspended breath as one lucky three-year-old earns the first prize on the road to a Triple Crown victory.

In order to understand how this single horse race captures the hearts of so many, and how the title became the most coveted win in the industry ... one needs to understand how it all began.

"Greatest Two Minutes in Sports"™

Thoroughbreds first started kicking up dirt in the Bluegrass state as early as 1783 when races were held on Market Street right through downtown Louisville. Fans later watched their favorite horses run between Main and 16th streets and even on an island in the Ohio River, called the Elm Tree Gardens.

Left: M.L. Clark and Family, M.L. Jr. on far right.
Kentucky Derby Museum

The Kentucky Derby was largely the creation of Colonel Meriwether Lewis Clark Jr. (1846-1899), the grandson of William Clark, of the famous Lewis and Clark expedition. In 1873, Clark was commissioned by wealthy Louisville businessmen and Bluegrass horse breeders to study successful racing ventures in England and France. This was a tall order. While Clark had experience in the banking and tobacco industries, the horse business was relatively new to him. In order to compensate, Clark, like his grandfather before him, set out on his own journey. He immersed himself in racetrack research by studying classic races, including the Epsom Oaks and Epsom Derby, both of which were nearly 100 years old at the time. Clark returned to form the Louisville Jockey Club in 1873 and the first public notice of the track was featured in the May 27, 1874 edition of the *Courier-Journal*.

Clark raised $32,000 to fund the track's construction by selling 320 membership subscriptions to the track at $100 each. He leased 80 acres of land from his wealthy uncles, Henry and John Churchill. For the inaugural race meet Clark patterned the three major stakes races: the Kentucky Derby, Kentucky Oaks, and the Clark Handicap after three major British races: the Epsom Derby, Epsom Oaks, and the St. Leger Stakes.

Above: Portrait, Meriwether Lewis Clark Jr.
Kentucky Derby Museum

On May 17, 1875, the track officially opened and began the tradition of the Kentucky Derby. For the estimated 10,000 in attendance, the opening day promised the excitement of four races on the card for Thoroughbred colts, and one race for their filly counterparts. At 1½ miles, the inaugural Kentucky Derby, the day's main attraction for three-year-old colts, was quite a bit longer than today's distance of 1¼ miles.

Above: Horse and buggy in front of Churchill Downs
R.G. Potter Collection, Photographic Archives, Courtesy of University of Louisville

Left: Early Churchill Downs Clubhouse
Courier-Journal and *Louisville Times*

The track originally featured a clubhouse, a porter's lodge, six stables, and a beautiful grandstand, which held up to 3,500 people. Unfortunately, there were two problems with the original grandstand. First, in the late afternoon, fans had to strain to see the finish line while staring into the setting sun. Second, a pleasant afternoon could be ruined by a shift in the wind, which brought unpleasant smells from the horse barns.

A new grandstand was constructed during the fall of 1894 through the spring of 1895 on the opposite side of the track at a reported cost of $100,000. The grandstand was adorned with two spires on its roof. Known as the Twin Spires, this elegant architectural element became known worldwide as the symbol of Churchill Downs and the Kentucky Derby.

Below: Churchill Downs Original Grandstand 1880s
Kentucky Derby Museum

Despite the enthusiasm that greeted the first Kentucky Derby, Churchill Downs was by no means an overnight success. Louisville tailor Matt J. Winn and a group of local investors took over the struggling track in 1902. As the Kentucky Derby grew in popularity, so did the racetrack. Under Winn's leadership, in 1903, Churchill Downs showed the first profit in its 28-year history. Matt Winn gave the Kentucky Derby an identity. He crafted many of its customs and developed Churchill Downs into a major entertainment venue.

Left: Matt Winn President of Churchill Downs from 1938-1949, Photo by H.C. Ashby, Official Turf Photographer © Churchill Downs, Inc./Kinetic Corporation

Below: Churchill Downs Grandstand, 1903
R.G. Potter Collection, Photographic Archives, Courtesy of University of Louisville

He is largely credited with creating many lasting traditions including: the playing of "My Old Kentucky Home" before the start of the Kentucky Derby, making the rose garland an integral presentation, commissioning the Kentucky Derby Gold Cup Trophy, and developing the mint julep glass, which remains a popular collectible souvenir to this day. Additionally, in 1925 Matt Winn facilitated the first broadcast of the Derby on network radio, effectively giving it a national presence.

As an entertainment venue under Winn's guidance, the first Kentucky State Fair was held at Churchill Downs. It featured a staged collision of two locomotives in front of a crowd of 40,000

Above: Churchill Downs dining room 1938-1949
© Churchill Downs, Inc./Kinetic Corporation

Left: 1920s Churchill Downs Entrance
Caufield & Shook Collection, Photographic Archives,
Courtesy of University of Louisville

Right (opposite page): Churchill Downs Expansion, 1920
Kentucky Derby Museum

to 50,000. Churchill Downs also witnessed automobile races held in the infield beginning in 1907. Although cars were a relatively new invention, speeds of up to 60 miles per hour were reported.

Matt Winn will forever be remembered as one of greatest allies the horse racing industry ever had. He established the Kentucky Derby as a premier American sporting event, with lasting traditions which are still a part of the Derby today. It seems fitting that the man who loved the Derby reportedly saw every one of the first 75 Derbys. One can only speculate the impact that first Derby had as the 13-year-old Winn watched from the back of his father's grocery wagon parked in the infield of Churchill Downs.

The First Derby

The winner of the very first Kentucky Derby was Aristides. He was a small, chestnut colt owned by the flamboyant, Kentucky-born, gaming house proprietor, H.P. McGrath. Ansel Williamson trained the horse and Oliver Lewis was the jockey. Aristides was initially thought of as the rabbit, the early race leader who sets the pace. H.P. McGrath entered the small colt into the Kentucky Derby to ensure a rapid pace, in hopes that his other entry Chesapeake, the favorite for the day, would take the win. However, the pace set by Aristides was so fast that by the far turn he was losing the rest of the field. Jockey Oliver Lewis eased up on his mount as instructed, but Chesapeake struggled to find his stride. McGrath urged Aristides on and Chesapeake finished eighth, making an exciting finish for the first Derby.

Right: Aristides, winner of the 1875 Kentucky Derby
© Churchill Downs, Inc./Kinetic Corporation

African-Americans *in Thoroughbred Racing*

African-Americans have played an important role in shaping horse racing in America. In the early days of our history, African-American slaves often assisted in the training of horses. Many were so insightful that they were given the responsibility of their masters' stable. It should come as no surprise that Ansel Williamson, trainer of the 1875 Kentucky Derby winner Aristides, was African-American. In fact, the 1876 and the 1877 Derby winners were also trained by African-Americans. In all, there have been 14 African-American trainers with entries in "the greatest race" and many have left their mark in the history books with tremendous finishes.

African-American jockeys have also played a vital role in American turf history. Oliver Lewis, the jockey of Aristides, went on to set an American record for 1½ miles on that fateful day in May. The next several decades saw African-Americans winning 15 out of the first 28 runnings of the Kentucky Derby. Some of the riders, like famed

Right: Isaac Murphy is considered to be one of the greatest jockeys in American history. He was the first jockey to win the Kentucky Derby on three occasions and on back-to-back runnings: Buchanan, 1884; Riley, 1890; and Kingman, 1891. Keeneland Library, Hemment Collection

jockey Isaac Murphy, rode back-to-back winners, as he did with Riley in 1890 and Kingman in 1891.

African-Americans have also impacted Kentucky Derby history in an ownership position. This role dates as far back to 1891 when Dudley Allen's horse Kingman won the 17th running of the Kentucky Derby. Today, you are likely to find African-Americans still interested and involved in Thoroughbred racing. Legendary Motown founder and Thoroughbred owner Berry Gordy finished in 8th place with his horse Plowis Castle in 1994. In 1989, trainer Hank Allen's Northern Wolf finished in 6th place.

Above: Kentucky Derby Winner, Kingman
Kentucky Derby Museum

Left: African-American trainer Hank Allen with Northern Wolf,
1989 Kentucky Derby
Kentucky Derby Museum

Left (opposite page): William Walker, African-American jockey who won
the 1877 Kentucky Derby with Baden-Baden who was trained by
African-American trainer Ed Brown.
Kentucky Derby Museum

Far Left (opposite page): Portrait of African-American jockey Isaac Lewis
aboard Montrose
© Churchill Downs, Inc./Kinetic Corporation

Women in Thoroughbred Racing

Throughout the late nineteenth and twentieth centuries, women have had an active role in Thoroughbred racing. The Kentucky Derby is no exception. Josephine Clay became the first woman to breed a Derby winner, Riley, in 1890. In 1904 Laska Durnell nominated her horse Elwood to the Derby, but kept his nomination a secret from her husband, Charles. Her surreptitious action worked out very well, as Elwood won as the longest shot in a field of five. His win was an important one, as it marked the first time a Kentucky Derby starter was owned by a woman. Additionally, his victory marked the second winner bred by a woman, Mrs. J.B. Prather.

Above: Penny Chenery, owner of Riva Ridge photographed with trainer Lucien Laurin after Riva Ridge's win in the 1972 Kentucky Derby.
Kentucky Derby Museum

In the 1940s, it was quite common to see a woman owner cheering on her horse at the Kentucky Derby and entering the Winner's Circle victoriously. At the 68th Kentucky Derby in 1942, seven of the eight finishers were owned by women. In all, female owners have won an impressive 21 Kentucky Derbys.

Women continue to serve the sport as trainers and jockeys. Female trainers have accounted for twelve Kentucky Derby starters, beginning in 1937 with Mary Hirsch, the daughter of legendary trainer Max Hirsch. Mary trained Derby starter No Sir, who finished 13th. After her showing at the Derby she again made history the next year, as she became the first woman to train a winner of the esteemed Travers Stakes at the Saratoga Race Course. Since Mary Hirsch's time, women trainers have sent 13 horses to post on Derby Day.

Female jockeys have also impacted the Kentucky Derby. In 1970, Diane Crump was the first woman to race in the Derby. Her horse, Fathom, finished 15th. Crump was also influential as she was the first woman to ride in a *pari-mutuel* race in North America in 1969 at Hialeah Park in Florida. Crump later became a trainer and rode for her own stable. Since the sport became open to women in 1969, five female jockeys have ridden in the Kentucky Derby.

Below: Diane Crump, first female to ride in a Kentucky Derby, finished 15th in 1970 aboard Fathom.
Courtesy of Photography, Inc. Louisville, Kentucky

Moments in Racing

Left: Kentucky Derby Winner Burgoo King
Kentucky Derby Museum

Below: This is an image of the solid gold set valued at
$7,000.00 (at the time) given by Churchill Downs and
the Kentucky Jockey Club to the winner of the 1922
Kentucky Derby, Morvich. Morvich was owned by Ben
Block, trained by Fred Burlew, and was ridden by jockey,
Albert Johnson. This trophy set preceded the traditional
Kentucky Derby Gold Cup Trophy, and like the
Kentucky Derby Trophy (Gold Cup) it was an idea
credited to the legendary Matt Winn.
Kentucky Derby Museum

Left: The Fighting Finish 1933 – Jockeys Herb Fisher aboard Head Play and
Don Meade aboard Brokers Tip. As the jockeys fought down the stretch it
was near impossible to tell who won the race, as this was before the days of
moving film patrol. That fateful decision rested with four stewards who
watched the race through binoculars and awarded Brokers Tip the winner.
For 32 years, this controversial decision prevented both jockeys from shaking
hands and making up as each one stuck to their version of the race.
Photo by Wallace Lowry
Courtesy of the *Courier-Journal*

The Kentucky Derby Trophy

The Kentucky Derby Gold Cup Trophy is a gold cup with a rich history. Awarded to the winning horse's owner each year, the trophy is made of 14-carat gold and weighs nearly four pounds, excluding its jade base. Smaller sterling versions are also presented to the winning trainer, jockey, and breeder.

Below: Trophy Set
© Churchill Downs, Inc./Kinetic Corporation

Right: The 75th Anniversary Kentucky Derby Trophy, 1949. This trophy, along with the 1974 and 1999 trophy featured jeweled embellishments, added to commemorate special anniversaries.
© Churchill Downs, Inc./Kinetic Corporation

Above: 1999 Kentucky Derby Gold Cup Trophy, with jeweled embellishments to celebrate the 125th running.
Kentucky Derby Museum

Prior to 1922, the winning owner took home a prize purse but only sporadically received trophies of any kind. In 1922, this was addressed by Churchill Downs as they awarded a gold buffet service set to Ben Block, the owner of the winning horse Morvich. Included in this service was a pair of candlesticks and a loving cup. In 1923, when Zev won the Derby, his owners were presented with the first version of the trophy. Black Gold, the 1924 winner, was presented with the "Golden Anniversary Trophy", which became the current design standard of the award given to the horse owner today.

The Kentucky Derby Gold Cup Trophy is one of the few solid gold trophies still awarded in an American sporting event. Since 1975, the trophy has been crafted by New England Sterling located in Attleboro, Massachusetts. It is formed from a brick of 14-carat gold and adorned with gold accents. The trophy, in the hands of master craftsmen, takes months to produce. Over the past 80 years, there have been slight variations to the design: diamonds were added to the horseshoe to celebrate the 75th running with Ponder. For the 125th celebration in 1999, rubies, diamonds, and emeralds were used as additional embellishments. 1999 also marked the year that the horseshoe, which adorns the front of the trophy, was changed from facing downwards to upwards. Racing superstition dictates that if the horseshoe is turned down all the luck will run out.

The Kentucky Derby Rose Garland

Roses have played an important role in Kentucky Derby traditions since the late nineteenth century. In 1883, racetrack lore tells of society ladies who attended a lively Louisville party and were presented with roses as gifts. This gift of flowers created a stir with the ladies and by the next year track president Col. M. Lewis Clark decided to feature the rose as the official flower of the 1884 Kentucky Derby.

Although 1884 marked the establishment of the rose as a tradition, the first published account of roses draped on the winning horse came in 1896 when Ben Brush was presented with an arrangement of white and pink roses tied with magenta and white ribbon. For the next several years horses were adorned with flowers, but often they were not roses, as in the case of the 1902 winner, Alan-a-Dale, who was festooned with carnations and ferns. Rose garlands were employed but they varied widely in appearance from year to year.

In 1931, Churchill Downs requested a standard pattern for the garland, and Louisville floral shop owner Mrs. Kingsley Walker designed and produced a complex pattern using over 500 dark red roses and greenery stitched onto a cloth-backed blanket. This design was introduced to the world by the 1932 Derby winner Burgoo King. Mrs. Walker retired in 1974 but her daughter Betty Korfhage continued the tradition until she sold the shop in 1984. Today, the Korfhage family continues to have a presence in the garden industry, as they operate a successful Louisville nursery and landscape company. [14] *(www.boardmansilversmith.com)*

Right: 1913 Kentucky Derby Winner Donerail
Kentucky Derby Museum

Since 1987, the garland has been in the hands of the master floral designers from Kroger, the national grocery chain. Today the garland is 2½ yards long, 14 inches wide, and weighs approximately 40 pounds. Each of the over 400 roses used in the garland are considered prime roses. Since each rosebush can produce only one prime rose, many rosebushes are necessary for the creation of the garland. The garland's lining is made of a rich, green satin stitched with the Twin Spires logo at one end and the seal of the Commonwealth of Kentucky on the other end.

The center of the garland is made up of a crown of roses and features the same number of roses as horses competing in the Kentucky Derby. A single rose in the crown's center is raised above the rest which symbolizes the struggle and heart of a Derby winner.

Each rose that makes up the garland is inserted into its own water vial and the vials remain hidden inside the lining. The blanket is still hand sewn, which allows for each rose to be prominent, effectively making for a dramatic presentation.

The delicate operation of sewing roses to the garland begins at 4 p.m. on the day before the Derby. This process is a public event and the crew prepares the garland at a Louisville Kroger store for all to see and appreciate. The crew works 10 to 12 hours to finish the process. A "Jockey's

Bouquet" featuring 60 matching long-stemmed roses wrapped with red ribbon is also created the evening before the Derby.

While fans enjoy the spectacle and the imagery of the rose garland, many horses do not. Some are spooked by the roses draped over their back and it can make for a nervous ceremony in the Winner's Circle.

Below: Secretariat 1973 Derby winner in the Winner's Circle with his groom, Eddie Sweat and jockey Ron Turcotte.
© Churchill Downs, Inc./Kinetic Corporation

Jockeys

Pound for pound, jockeys are among the world's strongest athletes. Tipping the scales lightly between 105-112 lbs., they tightly grip 1,200-pound Thoroughbreds as they thunder around racetracks at speeds of nearly 40 miles an hour. Crouching in a tight position over their horse, balancing lightly on their toes, jockeys are shot from the starting gates as their horses lunge forward. Looking for openings, steering without brakes, switching the whip from hand to hand, and getting bumped are all part of the job. A quick lean just a few inches to the side could result in a fatal, career-ending fall. These men and women are highly skilled, competitive athletes who sometimes compete in more than six races a day. Riding a thin line between risk and reward with percentages of the winnings only going to the top finishers, a jockey's livelihood can swing quickly between feast and famine. No matter the rest of his or her career, a victory in the Kentucky Derby ensures a jockey's name in the record books. For many, a win in the Derby is the ultimate accomplishment.

Top Left (opposite page): 1953 Kentucky Derby jockeys before the race
Kentucky Derby Museum

Top Right (opposite page): Eddie Arcaro congratulating Bill Shoemaker after his 1955 victory aboard Swaps
© Churchill Downs, Inc./Kinetic Corporation

Bottom Right (opposite page): Churchill Downs Jockey Quarters, 1930
Kentucky Derby Museum

Above: Pat Day jockey on Derby winner Lil E. Tee, 1992 Kentucky Derby
© Churchill Downs, Inc./Kinetic Corporation

Moments in Racing

Bugle start of the 1992 Kentucky Derby
© Churchill Downs, Inc./Kinetic Corporation

Great Thoroughbreds

Secretariat is considered one of the best horses of the twentieth century. In 1973, Secretariat became the first horse in 25 years to win the Triple Crown, setting records in many of his races. He was an extraordinary horse who could finish a race at a blistering pace. In the Kentucky Derby he came from last place to win, and he won the Belmont Stakes by 31 lengths. As a stud, he sired such future champions as 1988 Preakness and Belmont winner, Risen Star, and 1986 Horse of the Year Lady's Secret.

Right: Secretariat after his 1973 victory in the Kentucky Derby. In the Winner's Circle: Penny Chenery (owner), Lucien Laurin, (trainer) and Eddie Sweat (groom). Kentucky Derby Museum

Calumet Farm and Bull Lea

Below: Iron Liege 1957 Derby winner
© Churchill Downs, Inc./Kinetic Corporation

Calumet Farm, the most successful farm in Derby history, has bred and raced an outstanding record of eight Derby winners. Of these champions, three were sired by Bull Lea who was purchased for the relatively low price of $14,000 at a 1936 Saratoga racing auction. Bull Lea floundered a bit early on, finishing 8th in the 1938 Kentucky Derby. However, in his four-year-old season the colt became a champion racehorse with lifetime earnings of $94,825. Despite his eventual racing success, this late bloomer's true gift turned out to be in the breeding shed. He served as the number-one sire of Calumet by giving the world the 1948 Triple Crown winner Citation. Bull Lea also sired Derby winners Hill Gail (1952) and Iron Liege (1957). Calumet Farm will always be remembered for their many victories, their racing silks of "devil's red" and blue, and their sire Bull Lea, who made so many of their notable wins possible.

Fashion

The Kentucky Derby has earned its reputation as a fashion playground for spirited racing enthusiasts the world over. The spectacular female fashion often seen at the Kentucky Derby dates back to the first race. Opulent feminized dress has played a large role in the history of the Kentucky Derby. Colonel M. Lewis Clark envisioned a racing environment that felt comfortable and luxurious, an event that would remind people of European horse racing. For him to accomplish this required careful consideration of America's taboos about gambling and, in particular, women's opposition to it. Gambling at this time was considered a sport of men in which genteel women of society would likely never participate. In order to spur success at the track, Clark had to overcome this taboo and create an atmosphere that ladies and their families would enjoy. Clark's idea was that if the ladies enjoyed themselves, they would be less likely to object to their husbands' choice of gambling as entertainment.

Louisville Jockey Club,
MAY, 1886.
DERBY DAY
TEN DAYS.
SPRING MEETING,
Commencing Thursday, May 14.

Right: 1886 Louisville Jockey Club Advertisement for the annual Spring Meeting Kentucky Derby Museum

Above: The fashionable daughters of Col. Matt Winn, early 1920s
Kentucky Derby Museum

Element At Kentucky's Turf Classic

FOR this meeting of the Flower of the Bluegrass and the Aristocracy of the Nation, Stewart's has anticipated every feminine desire. Beautiful attire and dainty accessories have been assembled from the Marts of the World. The

Above: 1920s Track Fashions
Kentucky Derby Museum

For a well-to-do late nineteenth and early twentieth-century woman, a day at Churchill Downs, especially Derby Day, was an opportunity to be seen in the latest fashions. In 1901, the review of the Kentucky Derby in the *Courier-Journal* stated:

"The seats in the grandstand were filled with gaily dressed women and men. The mass of green, pink, red, yellow, blue, all the colors of the rainbow, blending into one harmonious whole was as beautiful a sight as His Eminence in the lead."

What would these women have worn? Perhaps surprising to some, local women would have had the opportunity to purchase dresses and accessories from a talented group of Louisville-based seamstresses. The dresses in the late nineteenth through the early twentieth century would have emphasized a slimmer bustled silhouette than those of years past. The length of these dresses would have assuredly been long, covering the ankles. Due to the fact that the Kentucky Derby is in the spring, fabrics of lightweight silk would have been a good, warm-weather choice. A pair of gloves, a hat, and perhaps a parasol would have been appropriate and helpful accessories for fashionable as well as practical women.

As societal rules softened in the twentieth century, the definition of what was deemed appropriate underwent a transformation. In the 1920s, women at the Derby could be seen wearing dresses or more modern suits complete with jackets. Some of the jackets of the 1920s were roomy and accommodating while others were fitted. Hats and gloves were still very much *de rigueur*, and not particularly exceptional at the track. The 1930s and 1940s followed in the same vein, but during these decades the formal suit became more popular than the dress.

Left: Irene Dunne, Postmaster General Farley, and James H.R. Cromwell and party enjoy the Derby in 1940. Dunne, a popular film actress who was nominated for the Academy Award five times, personifies early 1940s glamour with her elegant hat, coat, and gloves. © Churchill Downs, Inc./Kinetic Corporation

Right: Col. Matt Winn with three of his daughters at the 1939 Kentucky Derby © Churchill Downs, Inc./Kinetic Corporation

The 1950s ushered in a renewed prosperity to postwar America and clothing styles reflected the changing times. At the Kentucky Derby well-dressed women were seen in chic suits with skirts that were either fitted to the body or billowed outward with the assistance of crinoline underskirts. Again, gloves and hats were still quite popular and part of a well-dressed woman's wardrobe.

Right: Attending in 1951 were the Duke and Duchess of Windsor, Phillip and his wife, Wallis Simpson. Both the Duke and Duchess were fashion icons, whose style was copied worldwide.
Kentucky Derby Museum

Right (opposite page): This crowd from 1959 shows an overall view of Derby attire.
© Churchill Downs, Inc./Kinetic Corporation

Left: 1940s fashion
Courtesy of *Courier-Journal* and *Louisville Times*

Above: 1940s fashion–Gen. J. Fred Miles and Party
Kentucky Derby Museum

Right: Image from movie *Black Gold*, honoring the 1924 winner, filmed at the 1946 Kentucky Derby
Courtesy of *Courier-Journal* and *Louisville Times*

Right: 1960s fashion
Courtesy of *Courier-Journal* and *Louisville Times*

The rules that guided much of twentieth-century culture seemed to be thrown out the window in the mid-to late 1960s. Though the Derby was still viewed as a most respectable event with women continuing to dress as such, a change in the standards of dress had occurred. Millionaire's Row opened in 1966 and society women wore increasingly louder hats in order to stand out in this highbrow crowd. This trend of bigger, more spectacular hats might have developed due to the fact that while society was loosening its grip on the hat and glove formality, the Kentucky Derby offered women a place to continue the old traditions. Patterns and prints were also brighter, and hemlines were defiantly raised, yielding a much different aesthetic from spectators than years before.

Above: Hat scene 1965
© Churchill Downs, Inc./Kinetic Corporation

Left: Fashionable women in hats at an early 1960s Kentucky Derby
Courtesy of Bud Kameniske

The 1970s and 1980s saw a return to the longer skirt, while retaining the casual attitude of the 1960s. From the 1990s to today, the spring dress has begun to replace the suit, especially for younger women. While gloves have faded from daily wear, a head at Derby is still best dressed with a hat. Hats tend to get more ostentatious and more expensive each year.

Left: 1966 Hat scene
© Churchill Downs, Inc./
Kinetic Corporation

Right: Race fan in festive hat
Photo © Christine George

The style of the infield today is a direct about-face from the attire in the clubhouse. Women traditionally wear lightweight sundresses, cotton skirts, or more frequently, shorts. No matter the outfit, the hat is a common component of many an infield spectator's attire. However, the infield hat is not particularly formal and folks are frequently seen in anything from comfortable ball caps to kitschy homemade creations. The Kentucky Derby has earned its reputation as a fashion playground for spirited racing enthusiasts the world over.

Left: Woman donning yellow blossomed hat for Derby
Photo © Christine George

Above: Typical infield hat
Photo © Christine George

The Infield Crowd

The infield of Churchill Downs is home to perhaps the most infamous scene of Derby celebrations. Raucous celebrating in the open space which is surrounded by the racetrack began with the race's inception. However, the late 1960s were the beginning of the wilder antics that

are now commonly associated with the Derby. The day's events resemble the atmosphere of the Super Bowl or the Indianapolis 500. Crowds of people begin to descend on Louisville the Friday night before Derby. The infield gates open at 8:00 a.m. and early-arriving folks, with tarps, folding chairs, and coolers in hand choose their spots for the day-long party.

Above Right: Typical infield scene, 1975
© Churchill Downs, Inc./Kinetic Corporation

Above: Infield woman
© Churchill Downs, Inc./Kinetic Corporation

Left: A recent look at the infield from the Grandstand on Derby Day
Photo © Christine George

The atmosphere of the infield is an uninhibited good time; no one much cares if they see a horse or hear "My Old Kentucky Home." This is not a scene for high heels and white suits. Many infielders routinely try to sneak alcohol through security in a variety of interesting ways. If it is a rainy day, chances are there will be mud wrestling. Simply put, the infield is a massive party for the young at heart.

Moments in Racing

Above: Ferdinand, 1986, with jockey Bill Shoemaker
© Churchill Downs, Inc./Kinetic Corporation

Left: Start of 2005 Kentucky Derby
© Churchill Downs, Inc./Kinetic Corporation

Celebrities

The famous have found their way to the Kentucky Derby since the race's inception. Many of the noteworthy names come from very diverse backgrounds of celebrity. The Derby has played host to notable politicians, actors, musicians, and sports figures. The Derby has also hosted both twentieth- and twenty-first-century United States Presidents, including Harry Truman, Lyndon Johnson, Richard Nixon, Gerald Ford, Jimmy Carter, Ronald Reagan, and both Presidents Bush. However, out of the eight mentioned, only Nixon attended while in office.

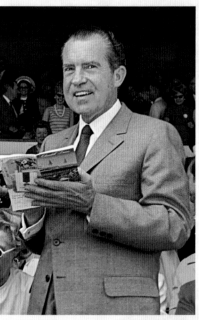

Above: President Richard Nixon. President Nixon is the only sitting President to attend a Kentucky Derby (1969). Other Presidents have attended the Derby as senators or governors: Harry S. Truman, Lyndon Johnson, governor George W. Bush who accompanied his father former President George Bush in 2000, Gerald Ford, Ronald Reagan, and Jimmy Carter. Kentucky Derby Museum

Left: Babe Ruth with John (Bud) Hillerich of Bradsby Bat Mfgrs. May 5, 1934 Kentucky Derby Kentucky Derby Museum

British royalty made the first appearance at the Derby with the arrival of the Seventeenth Earl of Derby, Mr. Edward George Villiers Stanley, in 1930. In 1951, the Duke and Duchess of Windsor followed in the tradition which brought Princess Margaret and her husband Lord Snowdon to the 100th running of the Derby. Derby goers in 2007 witnessed another royal year, with the arrival of Queen Elizabeth II and her husband Prince Phillip, Duke of Edinburgh.

The Kentucky Oaks

Col. Clark did not forget about the fillies when he created the Kentucky Derby. Instead, he made a race just for them, modeled after the Epsom Oaks of Great Britain. Vinaigrette was the winner of the first race that spanned the 1½-mile distance with a time of 2:39.75. Today's 1⅛-mile race is held the Friday before Derby and it attracts about 100,000 race fans. Many Kentuckians and Louisvillians consider the Kentucky Oaks a special racing day held just for them.

The Oaks has its own set of traditions as winners receive a garland of Stargazer Lilies, a trophy, and a set of 12 sterling silver julep cups. The winner's name is also engraved on the perpetual 25-inch sterling silver trophy, flanked by horse head handles on each side.

On exhibit at the Kentucky Derby Museum for all to see, the Oaks trophy is yet another tangible example of Matt Winn's lasting legacy; it has remained a venerable tradition since 1924.

Right: The Kentucky Oaks
© Churchill Downs, Inc./Kinetic Corporation

The Mint Julep

Since the Revolutionary War and the dawn of the American experience, Americans were quite busy consuming spirits. In 1792, the year Kentucky became a state, the average American including women and children consumed some 2½ gallons of spirits a year, with much of that consumption occurring before midday.

The julep's (or julap's) earliest English use was in the year 1400 when it was described as non-alcoholic medicinal concoction. By the mid-eighteenth century, a julep was a beverage made of spirits and in the United States, these spirits were topped with a sprig of fresh mint.

In addition to sugar, water, fresh mint, and crushed ice, Kentucky along with most of the post-bellum South preferred bourbon whiskey in their juleps. Mint juleps are generally made in this way today and are ideally served with straws and garnished with mint.

The mint julep has been the traditional beverage of Churchill Downs and the Kentucky Derby for nearly a century and each year almost 120,000 mint juleps are served during this two-day extravaganza. This is a feat that requires over 10,000 bottles of julep cocktail mix, 1,000 pounds of newly-harvested mint, and 60,000 pounds of crushed ice.

[5] *(Marty Godbey wrote the section entitled "Mint Julep" in* The Kentucky Encyclopedia, *edited by John E. Kleber and published by The University Press of Kentucky in 1992, page 641.)*

Right: Kentucky Derby mint julep glass, 1951
Kentucky Derby Museum

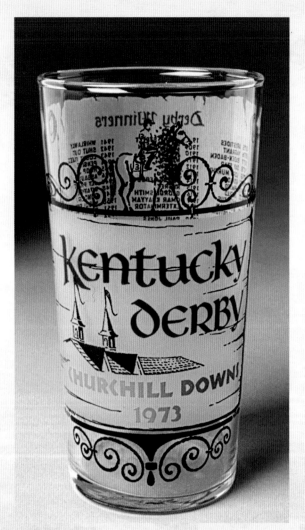

The history of the Kentucky Derby mint julep glass begins with unremarkable origins, as the first glasses were essentially water glasses. According to racetrack folklore, the glasses were so popular that they went missing from the tables in the track's dining rooms. Track management decided to charge dining room patrons an extra 25 cents if they wanted to keep the glasses.

Since its 1938 inception, the Kentucky Derby mint julep glass has grown in popularity and is often viewed as the leading Kentucky Derby collectible. As with many historic objects, the value of a Kentucky Derby glass is based in its rarity. From 1938 through 1952 less than 100,000 Kentucky Derby glasses were annually produced. In 1966, the production numbers rose to 250,000, shortly followed by an increase to 400,000 for the 100th running of the race in 1974. In 1985 the production run hit 500,000 and today it hovers around 700,000.

Until 1974, only Churchill Downs sold Derby glasses, making the limited supply the perfect collectible. However, after 1974, retail outlets began selling the glasses in honor of the 100th Derby.

Left: Kentucky Derby mint julep glass, 1973
Kentucky Derby Museum

In 1939, the Libbey Glass Company of Toledo, Ohio was contracted to create the glasses in color, which made them more eye-catching for mint julep sales. This change in design sparked great interest and reportedly tripled sales. Since that time, Libbey of Toledo, Ohio has manufactured nearly all of the Kentucky Derby mint julep glasses.

Over the years, some modifications have occurred. In 1940-1941, in a response to concern about broken glass found on the racetrack grounds, aluminum tumblers were introduced. During the war years of 1942-1944, aluminum was at a premium, so the Beetleware Company produced a ceramic-type tumbler in a variety of colors.

There have been many different designs on the glasses over the years. Generally the Twin Spires, the name Kentucky Derby, and racehorses are featured. The Kentucky Oaks race was honored with the first glass specifically marketed for the race in 2005 as the Libbey Company produced a limited order of 7,200. This roll has grown to a remarkable high of 606,824 in 2008.

Churchill Downs President Bill Corum introduced the sterling silver julep cups in 1951. The sterling silver julep cup was an idea of Col. Matt Winn, Corum's predecessor who died in 1949. Winn had discussed with Downs officials his opinion that there should be another official,

Right: Traditional sterling julep cup
Kentucky Derby Museum

useful souvenir of the Kentucky Derby.

The cups feature a small horseshoe and hold 12 fluid ounces. The julep cup plays an important role in Kentucky Derby folklore. Traditionally, the governor of Kentucky salutes the victorious Derby owner with a toast at the fashionable, invitation-only Winner's Party following the race.

Food at the Derby

The first Derby was an occasion for a picnic for many race goers. Nearby residents sold pralines, chicken, and fried fish from wicker baskets in the infield to hungry patrons. The amount of food served today at the Derby is truly astounding. Levy Restaurants serve a total of 7,000 pounds of beef, 1,000 pounds of pork, 63,000 shrimp, and 200,000 hot dogs.
The Derby experience would not be complete if patrons did not munch on at least one of the traditional foods that have become synonymous with the Derby. If you would like to preview some of the offerings, try some of these recipes:

Mint Julep Recipe

1 cup sugar
1 cup water
1 bunch fresh mint sprigs

• Crushed ice
• Kentucky Bourbon

Serves 8-10

Combine sugar and water and boil for 5 minutes, without stirring. Cool. Pour over a handful of mint. Refrigerate overnight in a closed jar. Remove mint leaves and continue to refrigerate. This will keep several weeks and individual juleps may be made as desired.

For each serving, fill an 8-ounce glass with crushed ice. Add one tablespoon syrup and one tablespoon water. Add 2 ounces bourbon. Stir gently until glass is frosted. Insert straw and garnish with a mint sprig.

Benedictine

Many Louisville hostesses are indebted to Jennie Benedict, a local caterer and restauranteur who invented this classic spread before the turn of the century. It is still served today at teas, brunches, and of course Derby parties. It can be used as a sandwich spread or as a tasty dip. *Yields 2 cups*

1 cucumber, peeled
1 medium onion
1 lb. cream cheese
2-3 drops of food coloring

Grate cucumber and onions (may use a food processor) and drain well in a strainer, pressing down with a spoon to remove all liquid. Discard liquid. Add drained cucumbers and onion to cream cheese and mix well in food processor. Color with 2-3 drops of green food coloring.

Mini Hot Browns

This dish originated in the 1920s at The Brown Hotel in Louisville, Kentucky. Though it is served throughout the year in Kentucky, it makes a special appearance during Derby time when nearly every restaurant features it on the menu. This is the perfect party appetizer. Recipe courtesy of the Café Musée. *Yields 18*

1   chicken bouillon cube
¼   cup of hot water
¾   cup half and half
3   T. unsalted butter
2   T. flour
1   cup grated Swiss cheese
5   strips of bacon cooked, crumbled
1   onion, sliced thin
6   oz. cooked turkey, thinly sliced
18 slices of party rye or
    small French bread
    parsley

Dissolve bouillon cube in hot water. Add half and half in a saucepan, melt butter and add flour. Whisk and cook until mixture is frothy and flour taste is gone. While stirring, add the bouillon mixture. Stir constantly with a whisk until the sauce thickens and begins to bubble. Add Swiss cheese and stir until smooth. (If sauce needs to be thinned, heat and add a little water.)

Assemble hot browns by placing turkey and onion on each bread slice. Top with sauce and crumbled bacon. Heat at 350 degrees for 10 minutes. Garnish with parsley.

"Kentucky Burgoo"

"Kentucky Burgoo" is the state's chosen stew. It is served at a variety of events from political rallies to church picnics and it is even a Derby Day favorite. In fact the 1932 winner Burgoo King was named after Lexington's J.T. Looney, one of Kentucky's most favorite Burgoo makers. This recipe is just the thing for a large crowd. *Serves 10*

1   large chicken
1-2   lbs. lean stew meat
      (beef, veal, and/or lamb)
3-4   pints of water
1½   tsp. coarsely ground
      pepper
½   tsp. cayenne pepper
2   small cans of tomato purée
12   potatoes
4   large onions
1   finely chopped head
      of cabbage
6-8   medium tomatoes,
      peeled and chopped
6-8   ears of fresh corn
1   lb. fresh carrots, sliced
1-2   T. salt
1   tsp. pepper
½-1   cup Worcestershire
      sauce

Cook chicken and other meat in water with coarsely ground pepper and cayenne pepper until chicken will leave the bones and the meat is very tender (40 minutes). Remove bones, shred meat and return to the liquid. Add tomato purée, potatoes, onions, cabbage, tomatoes, carrots and corn. Season with salt, pepper, and Worcestershire sauce. Cook slowly for 2-3 hours, until consistency of a thick stew, stirring from the bottom to keep from scorching. Add water, if necessary, to keep from sticking. If you like additional vegetables, add 2 cups of fresh sliced okra and/or 2 finely chopped green peppers.

"My Old Kentucky Home"

One of the most moving experiences in the world of sports is the playing of "My Old Kentucky Home" as the horses assemble on the track just moments before the start of the Kentucky Derby.

Nineteenth-century songwriter Stephen Foster wrote the ballad, but interestingly enough, he was not a native Kentuckian. Foster was born in Pennsylvania and grew up in Lawrenceville, a then-suburb of Philadelphia, as one of the youngest children in a large family. Despite the fact that he had very little formal music training, he was able to publish many well-known songs before the age of 20. Many of his songs like "Oh! Susana," "Camptown Races," and "My Old Kentucky Home" still remain popular over 150 years after their composition. Kentucky folklore points to Federal Hill in Bardstown, (the home of his distant cousins) as the inspiration for "My Old Kentucky Home."

No one can point to a definitive year that the Stephen Foster ballad became a tradition, but it was first mentioned in the *Courier-Journal* in the May 8, 1921 edition. In 1928, it became Kentucky's official song. Since 1936, barring a few exceptions, "My Old Kentucky Home"

has annually been performed by the University of Louisville Marching Band. Churchill Downs honors the famed composer with the Stephen Foster Handicap, the richest stakes race at the track outside of the Derby. It was created as a 1 1/8-mile race for three-year olds in 1982.

For anyone attending the Derby, especially a Kentuckian, the song is a point of pride and many Kentuckians know the tune by heart.

Right: Sheet Music, "My Old Kentucky Home" Kentucky Derby Museum

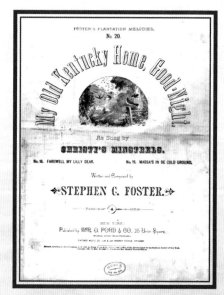

Birthdays

The foaling date of a horse is a good indicator of their maturity, which may affect the price he or she brings at auction. Though there is some disagreement, owners generally prefer an older foal, as they have more time to train and mature both physically and mentally. An older foal and his younger counterpart are often seen as the difference between a seventh-grade athlete competing against a rapidly maturing high school junior.

Rather than recording the actual birth date, for the ease of record keeping, the official birthday for all Thoroughbreds born in the Northern Hemisphere is January 1. In the Southern Hemisphere, it is July 1.

Most Derby winners were foaled in March or April. There are a few notable exceptions. Lawrin, the 1938 victor was a remarkably early foal as he was born on January 30, 1935. On the other end of the spectrum, there are a few Derby winners who were not actually three years old at the time that they ran for

the roses. Northern Dancer, the winner of the 1964 Derby was foaled on May 27, 1961 and the race was run on May 2, 1964. [3] *(Jim Bolus and Joe Hirsch. <u>Kentucky Derby: The Chance of a Lifetime.</u> New York: McGraw-Hill Book Company, 1988. page 26)*

Below: Lawrin, winner of the 1938 Kentucky Derby, was ridden by jockey Eddie Arcaro. © Churchill Downs, Inc./Kinetic Corporation

Moments in Racing

Above: 1995 Derby Thunder Gulch and Gary Stevens
© Churchill Downs, Inc./Kinetic Corporation

Left: At the races
Photo © Christine George

The Kentucky Derby Festival
&
The Governor's Breakfast

The Kentucky Derby Festival is an annual festival held in Louisville, Kentucky during the two weeks before the Run for the Roses. The festival is Kentucky's largest single annual event, with the first occurring in 1935.

The festival's first major event is Thunder Over Louisville, which is the largest fireworks display in the United States.

Each year, an official Derby poster is unveiled and prints are sold to help finance festival events. These events vary somewhat from year to year but they almost always include numerous athletic events, luncheons, private parties, fashion shows, wine tastings, and other lighthearted festivities.

Above: Thunder Over Louisville

It is a Derby Day tradition for Kentucky's sitting governor to entertain everyone who makes it to the mansion for the Governor's Breakfast. This event began on Derby morning in 1936 when Governor A.B. "Happy" Chandler and his wife Mildred, invited about 100 people to eat breakfast with them at the Governor's Mansion in Frankfort, about an hour east of Louisville. Decades later, the tradition continues and the menu still features Southern favorites: ham, grits, biscuits, and eggs. The event has evolved into a public affair with all visitors welcomed to a meal full of Kentucky charm.

In 2007, 17,000 people enjoyed breakfast and viewed exciting live entertainment. Typically, the event winds down around 11 a.m. and many of the revelers make their way down the Interstate to the Derby.

Right: Governor's Breakfast
Courtesy of Kentucky Office
of Creative Services

Churchill Downs Today

Churchill Downs is still one of the most successful racetracks in America. Its live racing calendar runs over 60 days per year over two separate meets: late April to early June and late October to late November. The track is available for training approximately 295 days per year. Over the years, various expansions have occurred. The latest renovations were complete for the 2005 Kentucky Derby and included 15 Finish Line Suites, an expanded Millionaire's Row, indoor box seating, and new dining and entertainment areas. The construction increased the permanent seating capacity from 48,500 to 52,000 at an estimated cost of $121 million.

Featured renovations:

Finish Line Suites
Expanded Millionaire's Row
Indoor Box Seating
New Dining and Entertainment Areas

A wide variety of seating at varying prices is offered for the Kentucky Derby. Millionaire's Row is the scene of celebrities and high ticket prices. On the other end of the spectrum sits the infield which is home to 80,000 revelers and rivals only Bourbon Street during Mardi Gras in its tradition and wild atmosphere.

Left: Commemorated in the courtyard garden, is Aristides, the first winner of the Kentucky Derby in 1875.
Kentucky Derby Museum

Bottom: 2005 Kentucky Oaks Churchill Downs
Kentucky Derby Museum

The Kentucky Derby Museum

The Kentucky Derby Museum, which sits on the front steps of historic Churchill Downs, is a very visible part of our community as one of Louisville's premier attractions. Graciously welcoming over 200,000 guests through the doors each year and giving them a firsthand look at the event for which Louisville, Kentucky is known worldwide, the Museum aims to provide a lasting impression of tradition, hospitality, and pride to our many visitors.

The Kentucky Derby Museum, in addition to preserving the history of the Kentucky Derby, offers so much more to our community. Through our Education Department, we offer a free children's program to all public and parochial schools within the states of Indiana and Kentucky. Our Outreach Program travels to communities within our state to educate Kentucky youth about the economics, history, and significance of the Kentucky Derby.

Opening to the public in April 1985, the Kentucky Derby Museum sits on land that Churchill Downs donated to the non-profit

Above: Visitors to the Museum get an up-close perspective of a variety of Derby elements.
Kentucky Derby Museum

corporation. The construction of the facility and seed money for the endowment fund was provided by the J. Graham Brown Foundation and five banks in the community. Although the Museum maintains a strong relationship with Churchill Downs, it functions as an entirely separate entity with self-generating revenue for its non-profit operating budget.

The Museum has welcomed more than 3.7 million visitors from all over the world including celebrities Bo Derek, Steven Spielberg, Kate Capshaw, Muhammad Ali, Sigourney Weaver, Gene Simmons, Susan St. James, Dick Eversoll, and President Mikhail Gorbachev.

The Museum's revenue is generated by visits to the Museum, gift shop sales, and rental income but further relies on generous sponsorships and grants from the community.

Photo © Churchill Downs, Inc./Kinetic Corporation

Conclusion

Traditions are an enduring part of the charm of the Kentucky Derby, and they range from the silly to the sublime. We have selected some of the most popular and venerable traditions.

We hope your interest in our traditions will inspire you to throw that Derby party, start your own collection of julep glasses, or perhaps you will even get misty-eyed the next time you hear "My Old Kentucky Home."

The Kentucky Derby Museum thanks you for purchasing this book. If you have any further questions please go to our website at **www.derbymuseum.org**

We will SHARE the FUN of the KENTUCKY DERBY EXPERIENCE!

A 501(c)3 non-profit corporation.

Bibliography

1. Badejo, Deidre. "African Americans In Thoroughbred Racing." Kentucky Humanities Council, Kentucky Derby Museum, 1993.
2. Bolus, Jim. Run For The Roses: 100 Years At The Kentucky Derby. New York: Hawthorn Books, Inc. 1974.
3. Bolus, Jim and Joe Hirsch. Kentucky Derby: The Chance of a Lifetime. New York: Mc Graw-Hill Book Company, 1988.
4. Chew, Peter. The Kentucky Derby: The First 100 Years. Boston: Houghton Mifflin Company, 1974.
5. Godbey, Marty. "Mint Julep" The Kentucky Encyclopedia, Lexington: The University Press of Kentucky, 1992.
6. Halladay, Jessie. "Feeding Derby fans' frenzy for food." USA TODAY 4 MAY 2006, natl.ed.
7. Harwell, Richard Barksdale. The Mint Julep. Charlottesville: University of Virginia Press, 2005.
8. The Kentucky Derby Museum. The Kentucky Derby Museum Cook Book. Louisville: Commercial Lithographing Company, 1992.
9. Kleber, John. The Kentucky Encyclopedia. Lexington: The University Press of Kentucky, 1992.
10. Kleber, John. The Encyclopedia of Louisville. Lexington: The University Press of Kentucky, 2000.
11. Mulvey, Kate. Decades of Beauty: The Changing Image of Women, 1890s-1990s. New York: Checkmark Books, 1998.
12. Thomas, Pauline Weston. "Victorians-1990s." Fashion-Era.com. http://www.fashion-era.com/index.htm.
13. 2008 Churchill Downs Media Guide. Louisville: Churchill Downs, 2008.
14. "Rose Garland History." Boardman Silversmiths. www.boardmansilversmiths.com/churchilldowns-boardman/rosegarlandhistory.htm.
15. "African Americans in the Derby." Churchill Downs. www.kentuckyderby.com/2009/history/african-americans-derby.
16. "Derby Connections." Churchill Downs. www.kentuckyderby.com/2009/history/connections.
17. "Kentucky Derby Festival History." Kentucky Derby Festival. www.kdf.org/History.html.
18. "Secretariat History." Secretariat.com www.secretariat.com/secretariat_history.htm.
19. "Timeline." Churchill Downs. www.kentuckyderby.com/2009/history/timeline.
20. "American Cultural History 1900-1990." Lone Star College Kingwood. 2009 Lone Star College. http://kclibrary.lonestar.edu/decade80.html.